Best of
McCall's QUILTING

Make Your First Quilt

You can do it! If you can sew a straight line, you can make beautiful quilts, and *McCall's Quilting* will show you how. Whether your style is traditional or modern, colorful or subdued, you'll find projects here too tempting to resist.

Go from nervous newbie to confident quilter with this unique 16-pattern collection.

LEISURE ARTS
the art of everyday living
www.leisurearts.com

Best of McCall's QUILTING

MAKE YOUR FIRST QUILT

EDITORIAL

Editor-in-Chief	**Beth Hayes**
Art Director	**Ellie Brown**
Senior Editor	**Kathryn Patterson**
Associate Editor	**Sherri Bain Driver**
Assistant Editor	**Erin Russek**
Web Editor	**Valerie Uland**
Administrative Editor	**Susan Zinanti**
Graphic Designers	**Karen Gillis Taylor**
	Tracee Doran
	Joyce Robinson
Photography Stylist	**Ashley Slupe**
Photographer	**Mellisa Karlin Mahoney**

CREATIVE CRAFTS GROUP, LLC

President & CEO	**Stephen J. Kent**
CFO	**Mark F. Arnett**
SVP, General Manager	**Tina Battock**
VP, Publishing Director	**Joel P. Toner**
SVP, Chief Marketing Officer	**Nicole McGuire**
VP, Production	**Barbara Schmitz**
Corporate Controller	**Jordan Bohrer**
Product & Video Development	**Kristi Loeffelholz**

OPERATIONS

Circulation Director	**Deb Westmaas**
New Business Mgr.	**Lance Covert**
Renewal & Billing Mgr.	**Nekeya Dancy**
Newsstand Consultant	**T. J. Montilli**
Digital Marketing Mgr.	**Laurie Harris**
Online Subscription Mgr.	**Jodi Lee**
Director of IT	**Tom Judd**
Production Manager	**Dominic Taormina**
Ad Prod. Coordinator	**Sarah Katz**
Advertising Coordinator	**Madalene Becker**
Administrative Assistant	**Jane Flynn**
Retail Sales	**LaRita Godfrey,** **800-815-3538**

ADVERTISING

Publisher	**Lisa O'Bryan,** **303-215-5641**
Advertising	**Cristy Adamski,** **715-824-4546**
Online Advertising	**Andrea Abrahamson,** **303-215-5686**

EDITORIAL OFFICES

McCall's Quilting
741 Corporate Circle, Suite A, Golden, CO 80401
(303) 215-5600 (303) 215-5601 fax

Produced by the editors of
McCall's Quilting magazine
for
Leisure Arts, Inc.
5701 Ranch Drive, Little Rock, AR 72223-9633
www.leisurearts.com.
Library of Congress Control Number: 2013937085
ISBN-13/EAN: 978-1-4647-0862-6

Contents

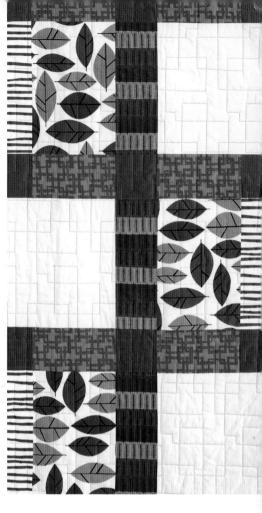

The twists and turns of any long wait in line are easy to see in this simple, stylized design. Select any five feature prints and a background fabric, and you're on your way…no need to take a number!

Cafeteria Line

Designed by
MARNY BUCK
and JILL GUFFY
of Modern Quilt Relish

Machine Quilted by
APRIL WEST

Finished Quilt Size
60½″ x 76½″

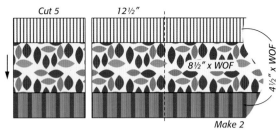
Cut 5   12½"

8½" x WOF

4½" x WOF

Make 2

Diagram I-A

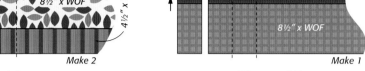
Cut 8   4½"

4½" x WOF

8½" x WOF

Make 1

Diagram I-B

Fabric Requirements

Cream/brown stripe **and** brown solid (piecing)	⅜ yd. **each**
Cream/multicolor leaf print (piecing)	⅝ yd.
Green/blue stripe (piecing, binding)	1⅛ yds.
Green grid print (piecing)	½ yd.
Cream solid (background)	2⅞ yds.
Backing (piece lengthwise)	4⅞ yds.
Batting size	70" x 86"

Planning

Cream solid fabric is the perfect background for cool contemporary prints. The piecing is super-easy, leaving you time to add modern machine quilting to highlight the open areas of the quilt.

Cutting Instructions

(cut in order listed)

Cream/brown stripe
  2 strips 4½" x width of fabric (WOF)
Cream/multicolor leaf print
  2 strips 8½" x WOF
Green/blue stripe
  2 strips 4½" x WOF
  8 strips 2½" x WOF (binding)
Brown solid
  1 strip 4½" x WOF
  4 squares 4½" x 4½"
Green grid print
  1 strip 8½" x WOF
  1 strip 4½" x 20½"
  1 strip 4½" x 12½"
Cream solid
  3 strips 12½" x 32½"
  2 rectangles 12½" x 24½"
  2 rectangles 12½" x 20½"
  3 squares 12½" x 12½"
  3 strips 4½" x 20½"
  3 strips 4½" x 12½"

Piecing the Segments and Quilt Top

❶ Sew together 1 each cream/brown stripe, cream/multicolor leaf print, and green/blue stripe WOF strips in sizes and arrangement shown in **Diagram I-A**. Make 2. Press seams in direction of arrow. Cut 5 segments 12½" wide. In similar manner, make strip set shown in **Diagram I-B**, press, and cut 8 segments 4½" wide.

❷ Referring to the **Assembly Diagram** and watching orientation of segments, sew 9 rows using cream solid patches, segments, remaining green grid print strips, and brown solid squares. Sew rows together.

Quilting and Finishing

❸ Layer, baste, and quilt. April used a silk batting, and machine quilted a repeating irregular grid using olive green thread. Bind with green/blue stripe.

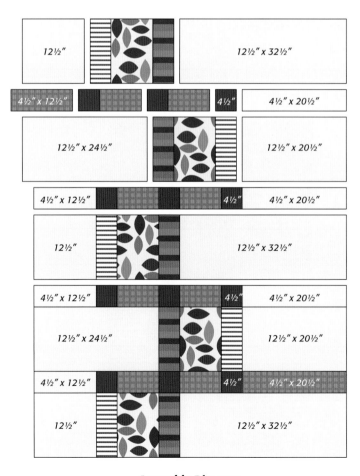

Assembly Diagram

Wonderful textured fabrics give this simple design depth and interest. The woven look is created when blocks are rotated during assembly. It couldn't be easier!

Simply Strips!

Designed and Machine Quilted by
MICHELE SCOTT

Made by
ELINORE LOCKE

Finished Quilt Size
70″ x 80″

Number of Blocks and Finished Size
21 A Blocks
10″ x 10″
21 B Blocks
10″ x 10″

*Fabric Requirements

Light green **and** light blue (blocks)	1⅛ yds.
	each
#1 dark green (blocks, inner border, binding)	2¼ yds.
Tan (blocks)	1¼ yds.
Aqua (blocks)	½ yd.
#2 dark green (blocks)	1 yd.
Tan/green (outer border)	1⅛ yds.
Backing (piece lengthwise)	5⅛ yds.
Batting size	78″ x 88″

*All fabrics are stone-textured prints.

Planning
All blocks are cut from just 2 types of strip sets, making this a fast, easy design.

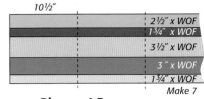

Diagram I-A

Cut 21   10½″

2¼″ x WOF
3″ x WOF
1¾″ x WOF
1¾″ x WOF
3″ x WOF
1¼″ x WOF

Make 7

Cut 21   10½″

2½″ x WOF
1¾″ x WOF
3½″ x WOF
3″ x WOF
1¾″ x WOF

Diagram I-B

Make 7

Cutting Instructions
(cut in order listed)

Light green
  7 strips 2¼″ x width of fabric (WOF)
  7 strips 2½″ x WOF

#1 dark green
  7 strips 3″ x WOF
  7 strips 1¾″ x WOF
  *4 strips 1½″ x 74″, pieced from 8 WOF
    strips
  9 strips 2½″ x WOF (binding)

Tan
  7 strips 1¾″ x WOF
  7 strips 3½″ x WOF

Aqua
  7 strips 1¾″ x WOF

Light blue
  7 strips 3″ x WOF
  7 strips 1¾″ x WOF

#2 dark green
  7 strips 1¼″ x WOF
  7 strips 3″ x WOF

Tan/green
  *4 strips 4¼″ x 76″, pieced from 8 WOF
    strips

*Border strips include extra length for trimming.

Piecing the Blocks

1 Referring to **Diagram I-A**, sew together 6 WOF strips of colors and sizes shown to make strip set. Make 7. Press all seams in direction of arrow. Cut 21 A Blocks 10½″ wide.

2 In similar manner, refer to **Diagram I-B** to make 21 B Blocks.

Assembling the Quilt Top

Note: Refer to **Assembly Diagram** for following steps.

3 Sew 7 rows of 6 blocks each, alternating A and B Blocks and rotating as shown. Sew rows together.

4 Stitch #1 dark green 74″ strips to sides. Press seam allowances away from quilt center, and trim strips even with top and bottom. Stitch remaining 74″ strips to top/bottom; press and trim even with sides. Sew tan/green 76″ strips to sides; press and trim even. Sew remaining tan/green strips to top/bottom; press and trim even.

Quilting and Finishing

5 Layer, baste, and quilt. Michele used Fairfield Bamboo batting and machine quilted a large meander. Bind with #1 dark green 2½″-wide strips.

Play with Color

Soft florals and other prints create a romantic feel in this version of Michele's easy design.

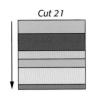

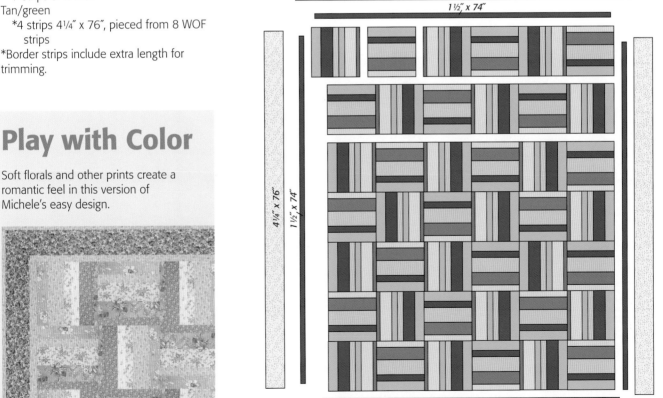

4¼″ x 76″

1½″ x 74″

4¼″ x 76″

1½″ x 74″

Assembly Diagram

Paradigm Shift

Designed by
JANELLE CEDUSKY

Machine Quilted by
SHELLEY NEALON
of Quilted Bliss

Try this fun, easy project with two-at-a-time block construction, and your approach to quilt design may never be the same!

Finished Quilt Size 52¼" x 60⅞"

Number of Blocks and Finished Size
42 Mock Log Cabin Blocks 8⅝" x 8⅝"

Fabric Requirements

Assorted white/black prints (blocks)	1⅝-2 yds. **total**
Lime solid (block centers)	⅝ yd.
Assorted black/white prints (blocks)	1⅝-2 yds. **total**
Black solid (binding)	¾ yd.
Backing (piece widthwise)	3½ yds.
Batting size	60" x 70"

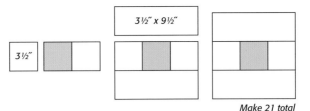

Make 21 total
Diagram I-A

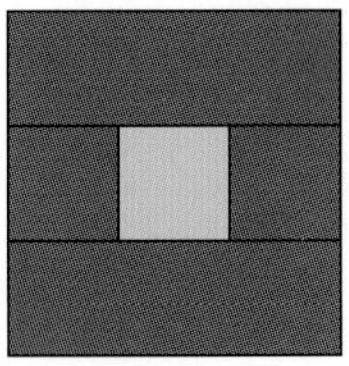

Make 21 total
Diagram I-B

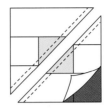

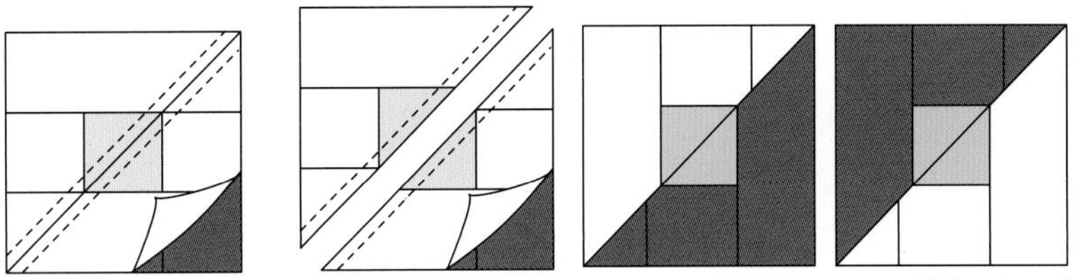

Make 42 total
Diagram II

Planning

Janelle made this fun contemporary quilt using black and white prints from her stash plus a splash of lime for a zesty accent. You'll love her quick and clever take on the traditional Log Cabin, and the energy of her asymmetrical block arrangement.

Cutting Instructions

Assorted white/black prints—**cut 21 matching sets of:**
  *2 strips 3½" x 9½"
  2 squares 3½" x 3½"
Lime solid
  42 squares 3½" x 3½"
Assorted black/white prints—**cut 21 matching sets of:**
  *2 strips 3½" x 9½"
  2 squares 3½" x 3½"
Black solid
  7 strips 2½" x width of fabric (binding)
*Cut first.

Piecing the Blocks

① Referring to **Diagram I-A**, sew matching white/black print 3½" squares to opposite sides of lime square. Stitch matching 9½" strips to top and bottom to make pieced square. Make 21 total. In same manner, make 21 total pieced squares using matching sets of black/white print patches and lime squares (**Diagram I-B**).

② Draw diagonal line on wrong side of white pieced square. Referring to **Diagram II**, place marked square on black pieced square, right sides together and with long seams of the pieced squares in opposite directions. Sew ¼" seam on each side of marked line; cut apart on marked line. Press open to make Mock Log Cabin Blocks. Make 42 total.

Assembly Diagram

Quilt Top Assembly

③ Referring to the **Assembly Diagram**, arrange and sew 7 rows of 6 blocks each, orienting blocks as shown. Sew rows together.

Quilting and Finishing

④ Layer, baste, and quilt. Shelley used lime-colored thread to machine quilt a continuous pattern of random-length horizontal and vertical straight lines. Bind with black solid.

Visit
McCallsQuilting.com
On our website you'll find patterns for pillows that coordinate with this quilt.

Explore Your Options

This country cousin of the featured quilt sports blocks with traditional red centers and homespun plaids.

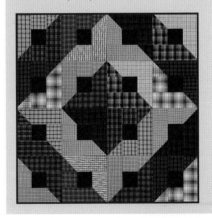

Big Print Bounty

Three sizes of squares

give this easy, sophisticated quilt a sense of movement and depth. Start with your favorite modern fabric collection and show it all off!

Designed by
ELLIE BROWN

Machine Quilted by
TRICIA CAMP

Finished Quilt Size
63½" x 84½"

Number of Blocks and Finished Sizes
28 Rectangular
    Blocks 9" x 12"
28 Four-Patch
    Blocks 9" x 9"

Planning and Cutting

McCall's Quilting art director Ellie Brown designed this quilt for her daughter, who loves bold modern fabrics and bright colors. Ellie used assorted fabrics from her stash; choose prints with different values (light to dark) and scale (small to large motifs) to get the same look as in the featured quilt. Note that when large prints are cut up, some patches cut from the same print may look like they were cut from a completely different fabric. This adds to the interest and fun.

Each vertical block row is made with 4 matching Rectangular Blocks and 4 matching Four-Patch Blocks. Odd-numbered vertical rows begin with a Rectangular Block, and even-numbered vertical rows begin with a Four-Patch Block.

Cutting Instructions

Assorted green, purple, pink, brown, gray, gold, and cream prints
  for large squares, cut 7 sets of:
    4 matching squares 9½″ x 9½″
  for Four-Patch Blocks, cut a total of:
    14 strips 5″ x width of fabric (WOF)
  for strip-pieced segments, cut a total of:
    19 strips 3½″ x 20-22″
Gray/lavender print
  9 strips 2½″ x WOF (binding)
  2 strips 3½″ x 20-22″ (for strip-pieced
    segments)

Piecing the Blocks

1 Sew together 3 assorted 3½" x 20-22" strips to make strip set (**Diagram I-A**). Make 7 total. Press seams towards darker fabrics. From each strip set, cut 4 segments 3½" wide. Sew segment to assorted 9½" square to make Rectangular Block (**Diagram I-B**). Make 7 sets of 4 matching.

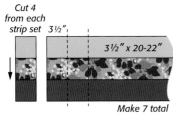

Diagram I-A

Cut 4 from each strip set 3½"

3½" x 20-22"

Make 7 total

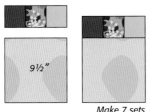

Diagram I-B

9½"

Make 7 sets of 4 matching

Assembly Diagram

2 Stitch together 2 assorted 5" x WOF strips to make strip set (**Diagram II-A**). Make 7 total. Press seams towards darker fabrics. From each strip set, cut 8 segments 5" wide. Sew together 2 matching segments to make Four-Patch Block (**Diagram II-B**). Make 7 sets of 4 matching.

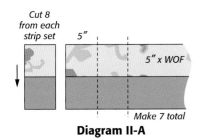

Diagram II-A

Cut 8 from each strip set 5"

5" x WOF

Make 7 total

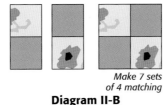

Diagram II-B

Make 7 sets of 4 matching

Assembling the Quilt Top

3 Referring to the **Assembly Diagram**, sew 4 vertical rows of 4 Rectangular and 4 Four-Patch Blocks each, alternating. Sew 3 vertical rows of 4 Four-Patch and 4 Rectangular Blocks each, alternating. Sew rows together as shown.

Quilting and Finishing

4 Layer, baste, and quilt. Tricia machine quilted an overall looping design. Bind with gray/lavender print.

Whether you start with a pack of precut 10″ fabric squares or yardage, this throw is as quick to make as it is lovely to look at. It's so pretty you may want to sew one for a friend, and one for you.

Cottage Whispers

Designed by
BETH HAYES

Made by
KATHY HANNAH

Machine Quilted by
BARBARA SHIE

Finished Quilt Size
60″ x 60″

**Number of Blocks
and Finished Size**
36 Hourglass Blocks
8½″ x 8½″

TO PRAY FOR ONE

Fabric Requirements

Assorted cream, green, blue, yellow, and pink prints (blocks, pieced border, pieced binding)	4⅛-4⅝ yds. **total***
Backing	4 yds.
Batting size	68" x 68"

*Or substitute 58 precut 10" fabric squares; see **Planning and Cutting**.

Planning and Cutting

If you use precut 10" fabric squares, cut 9¾" squares from 36 precuts, cut four 4¾" squares from each of 13 precuts, and cut binding strips from the remaining precut squares. Our instructions will lead you to make 36 sets of 2 matching blocks; place them randomly to get the same soft, unstructured look as in the original quilt.

Cutting Instructions
(cut in order listed)

Assorted cream, green, blue, yellow, and pink prints—**cut a total of:**

- 36 squares 9¾" x 9¾"
- 52 squares 4¾" x 4¾"
- 34 strips 2½" x 10" (pieced binding)

Piecing the Blocks

❶ Draw 2 diagonal lines on wrong side of assorted print 9¾" square. Place marked square on 9¾" square of a 2nd assorted print, right sides together (**Diagram I-A**). Sew ¼" seam on each side of one line. Cutting on unsewn line first, then on remaining drawn line, cut sewn square into quarters. Open and press to make 4 pieced triangles. Make 72 total.

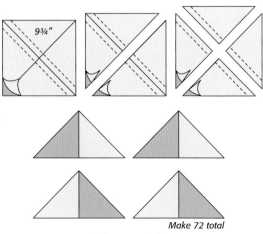

Make 72 total

Diagram I-A

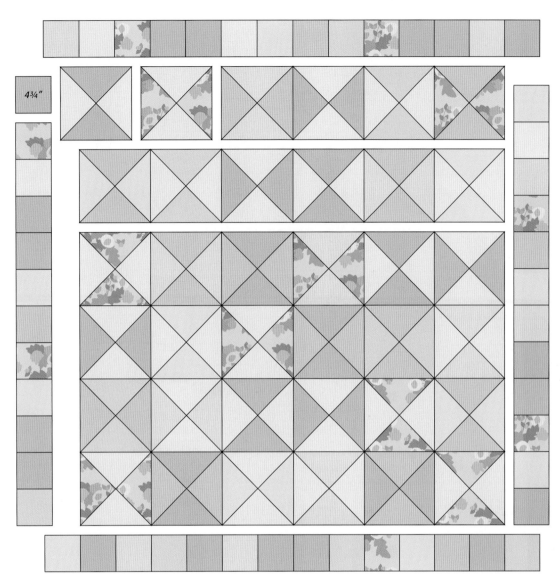

Assembly Diagram

② Sew together 2 matching pieced triangles to make Hourglass Block (**Diagram I-B**). Make 36 total.

Make 36 total

Diagram I-B

Assembling the Quilt Top
Note: Refer to **Assembly Diagram** for following steps.

③ Sew 6 rows of 6 blocks each. Sew rows together.

④ Sew together 12 assorted 4¾" squares to make side border strip. Make 2. Sew to sides. Sew together 14 assorted 4¾" squares to make top/bottom border strip. Make 2. Sew to top and bottom.

Quilting and Finishing
⑤ Layer, baste, and quilt. Barbara machine quilted an overall swirl design.

⑥ Using diagonal seams (**Diagram II**), sew together 34 assorted 2½" x 10" strips end to end. Bind quilt with pieced strip.

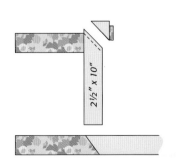

Diagram II

Egyptian Tablets

Clay tablets thousands of years old were the inspiration for this intriguing yet easy quilt design. Optional embroidery stitches are used for hand quilting…step-by-step photos show you how.

Designed by
VICKY WOSNIAK

Finished Quilt Size
61½" x 69"

*Fabric Requirements
5 assorted orange/rust prints/
   batiks (strip set A)   ⅜ yd. **each**
5 assorted cream/beige/
   black prints/batiks (strip
   set B)   ⅜ yd. **each**
4 assorted brown/rust/peach
   prints/batiks (strip set C)   ⅜ yd. **each**
Dark rust print (strip set C,
   outer border, facing)   2⅛ yds.
Black solid (strips, inner border) 1 yd.
Backing (piece widthwise)   4 yds.
Batting size   70" x 78"
*See **Planning.**

Planning

Careful fabric selection is key to the success of this quilt. The beauty and drama of the design come from having fabrics in each color group arranged in a run of values from dark to light or light to dark. Keep this in mind when choosing your fabrics; you may find it helpful to look closely at the photos.

Our instructions have you finish the quilt edges with a facing, as Vicky did. If you prefer, use the facing strips to finish your quilt with traditional binding instead.

Cutting Instructions
(cut in order listed)
5 assorted orange/rust prints/batiks—**cut from each:**
   4 strips 2" x width of fabric (WOF)
5 assorted cream/beige/black prints/batiks—**cut from each:**
   4 strips 2" x WOF
4 assorted brown/rust/peach prints/batiks—**cut from each:**
   4 strips 2" x WOF

Dark rust print
   *4 strips 3½" x length of fabric (LOF)
   *4 strips 2½" x LOF (facing)
   4 strips 2" x 40", cut on lengthwise grain
Black solid
   *7 strips 2" x 64", pieced from 14
     WOF strips
*Strips include extra length for trimming.

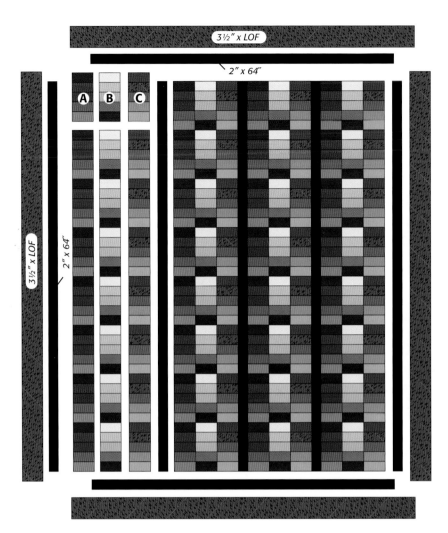

Making the Segments

1 Referring to **Diagram I** and arranging fabrics from dark to light, sew together 5 orange/rust WOF strips to make strip set A. Make 4. Press towards the darkest fabric; cut into 32 A segments 4½" wide. In similar manner make remaining strip sets; press. Cut 32 each B and C segments.

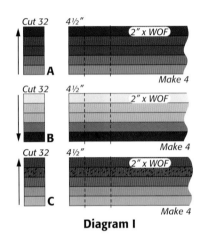

Diagram I

Assembling the Quilt Top

Note: Refer to **Assembly Diagram** for following steps, watching placement and orientation.

2 Sew together 8 A segments to make pieced strip. Make 4. In same manner make 4 each B-segment and C-segment pieced strips.

3 In order shown, stitch together 5 black 64" strips and 12 pieced strips, trimming black strips even after each addition. Stitch remaining black 64" strips to top and bottom; trim even with sides. Sew dark rust print 3½" x LOF strips to sides; trim even. Add dark rust 3½" x LOF strips to top/bottom; trim even.

Quilting and Finishing

4 Layer, baste, and quilt. Using multicolored thread, Vicky hand quilted black strips in the ditch and quilted along segment seams using Cretan stitch. To learn this stitch, see **Hand Quilting with Cretan Stitch**, next page.

Assembly Diagram

5 Trim quilt edges even. Press ¼" to wrong side along one long edge of each 2½" x LOF facing strip. Pin right sides of

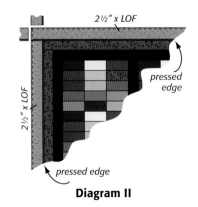

Diagram II

pressed strips to sides, top, and bottom of quilt front, aligning raw edges and overlapping at corners (**Diagram II**). Trim ends even. Stitch ¼" from quilt edge, through all layers, pivoting at corners. Trim corners. Turn facing to back of quilt; hand stitch pressed edges in place.

TIP

For help with hand quilting basics, visit **McCallsQuilting.com**, click on Lessons, and then Quilting...Hand.

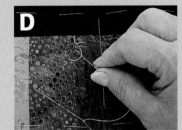

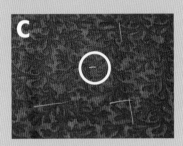

Hand Quilting with Cretan Stitch

Note: For this technique, begin by layering and basting quilt as usual. Contrasting thread is used in photos for clarity.

1 Thread needle and bury knot in batting at beginning of seam. Referring to **Photo A**, bring needle up just to left of seam. Keeping thread under needle, go down at a point that is approximately ¼" down and ¼" to right of seam. Being sure to stitch through all 3 layers of quilt sandwich, bring needle up just short of seam.

2 Gently pull needle through loop formed by thread until thread forms a right angle (**Photo B**). Stitch should show as short straight stitch on back of quilt (**Photo C**).

3 In similar manner, insert needle at a point approximately ¼" down and ¼" to left of seam. Bring needle up just short of seam and pull through thread loop as before (**Photo D**), forming a right angle (**Photo E**).

4 Continue stitching in this manner, forming stitches on alternating sides of seam (**Photo F**). Remove basting threads or pins as you approach them (**Photo G**). Check on back of quilt to be sure stitches are going through all layers (**Photo H**). When end of seam is reached, insert needle just where seam and black strip meet (**Photo I**). Knot thread and hide knot in batting as usual.

5 Feel free to alter stitch length and width as desired. If you're having trouble positioning stitches evenly, mark a removable line ¼" from seam for guidance. Always test for removability on a scrap of fabric before marking quilt. Remove marks when quilting is complete.

Soft, Sweet Stars

"Relax…dream…take comfort…renew…" Your version of this beautiful quilt will whisper all these things and more as you rest under its soft florals and subtle textural prints, combined in no-stress star blocks.

Designed by
GERRI ROBINSON

Machine Quilted by
REBECCA SEGURA
of Zeffie's Quilts

Finished Quilt Size 83½" x 99½"

Number of Blocks and Finished Size
80 Sawtooth Star Blocks 8" x 8"

Fabric Requirements

Assorted tan, yellow, pink, blue, and green florals (stars)	4¼-4½ yds. **total**
Assorted pink, blue, yellow, green, and tan textures (star backgrounds)	4⅜-4⅝ yds. **total**
Pink/cream print (border)	2¾ yds.*
Blue large floral (binding)	1¼ yds.*
Backing (piece widthwise)	7⅞ yds.
Batting size	92" x 108"

*See **Planning**.

Planning

One of the most basic guidelines of quilt design is to use fabrics with contrasting values, light to dark, for visual interest and to show off pieced work. But rules were made to be broken, and Gerri broke this one beautifully. The lack of contrasting values in the quilt creates a soft, watercolor effect, and draws the viewer in for a closer look.

If you like more contrast in your piecing, check out our black and white version of the design on page 26.

Gerri cut patches for a few star backgrounds from the border fabric, and patches for a few stars from the binding fabric. To do likewise, cut border and binding strips first, and then cut block patches as desired.

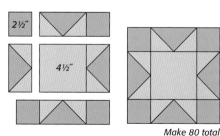

Explore Your Options

Scrappy stars in black and white prints with a few red accents lend drama to this easy quilt. A bold border print adds the perfect finish.

Cutting Instructions

Assorted tan, yellow, pink, blue, and green florals—**cut 80 matching sets of:**
  8 squares 2½" x 2½"
  1 square 4½" x 4½"
Assorted pink, blue, yellow, green, and tan textures—**cut 80 matching sets of:**
  4 rectangles 2½" x 4½"
  4 squares 2½" x 2½"
Pink/cream print
  4 strips 10" x 88", cut on lengthwise grain
Blue large floral
  11 strips 2½" x width of fabric (binding)

Piecing the Blocks

① Draw diagonal line on wrong side of assorted floral 2½" square. Place marked square on assorted texture 2½" x 4½" rectangle, right sides together, aligning raw edges (**Diagram I**). Sew on marked line; trim away and discard excess fabric. Press open. Repeat process, adding matching floral square to opposite end, to make pieced rectangle. Make 80 sets of 4 matching.

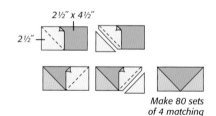

Make 80 sets of 4 matching

Diagram I

② Referring to **Diagram II**, sew 3 rows using 4 matching texture 2½" squares, 4 matching pieced rectangles, and matching 4½" square. Sew rows together to make Sawtooth Star Block. Make 80 total.

Make 80 total

Diagram II

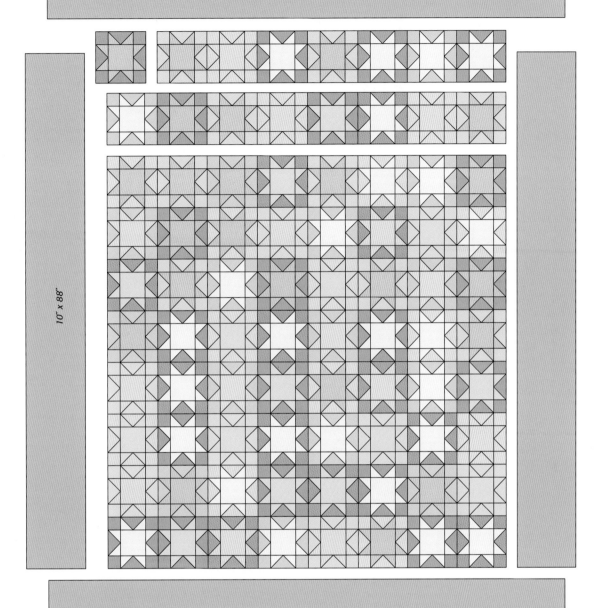

Assembly Diagram

Quilt Top Assembly

Note: Refer to **Assembly Diagram** for following steps.

③ Stitch 10 rows of 8 blocks each. Stitch rows together.

④ Sew pink/cream print 88″ strips to sides; trim even with top and bottom. Sew remaining pink/cream strips to top/bottom; trim even with sides.

Quilting and Finishing

⑤ Layer, baste, and quilt. Rebecca machine quilted curves on the star patches, and filled block backgrounds and part of the border with close, looping meanders. The rest of the border is quilted in a 4-strand swag, and straight lines perpendicular to the quilt edges, 1″ apart and ending at a curving line. Bind with blue large floral.

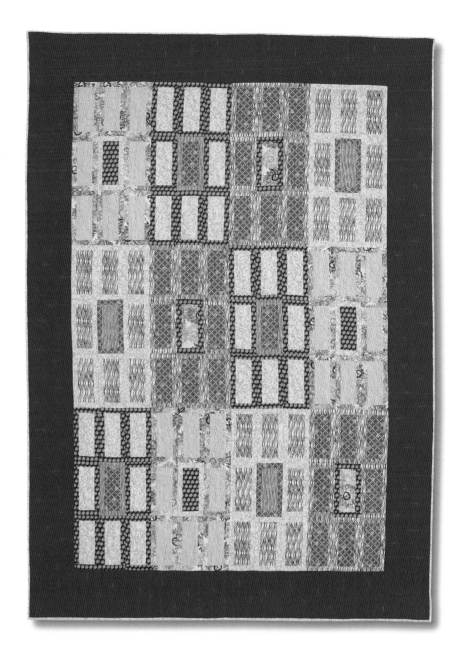

Designed by
LORI MASON

Made by
MARGARET A.
ROULEAU

Machine Quilted
by JULIE BEANE

**Finished Quilt
Size**
62½" x 86½"

**Number of Blocks
and Finished Size**
12 Open Window
Blocks 12" x 24"

Fabric Requirements

Blue/green large floral (blocks)	⅞ yd.
Yellow print (blocks)	⅝ yd.
Light blue print (blocks, binding)	2 yds.
Dark blue/green dot (blocks)	1 yd.
Blue stripe **and** blue multicolor print (blocks)	1¼ yds.* **each**
Blue small floral (blocks)	¾ yd.
Blue solid (border)	2¼ yds.
Backing (piece lengthwise)	5½ yds.
Batting size	72" x 96"

*Yardage and cutting based on
featured fabric.

Open Window

Master the strip piecing technique as you
make this appealing lap size quilt. **It's sew easy!**

Planning

Lori created a versatile design, lending itself to many different colors, prints, and themes.

Margaret used some directional fabrics, cutting patches so the pattern runs lengthwise in pieced rectangles. Follow our instructions to do the same.

Cutting Instructions

(cut in order listed)

Blue/green large floral
    10 strips 1¼" x width of fabric (WOF)
    1 strip 3" x WOF
    48 strips 1¼" x 4½"

Yellow print
    5 strips 3" x WOF

Light blue print
    9 strips 2½" x WOF (binding)
    12 strips 1¼" x WOF
    5 strips 3" x WOF
    54 strips 1¼" x 4½"

Dark blue/green dot
    1 strip 3" x WOF
    12 strips 1¼" x WOF
    54 strips 1¼" x 4½"

Blue stripe
    2 strips 1¼" x 40", cut on lengthwise grain
    1 strip 3" x 40", cut on lengthwise grain
    6 strips 1¼" x 4½", cut on crosswise grain

Blue small floral
    6 strips 3" x WOF
    2 strips 1¼" x WOF
    6 strips 1¼" x 4½"

Blue multicolor print
    10 strips 1¼" x 40", cut on lengthwise grain
    5 strips 3" x 40", cut on lengthwise grain
    48 strips 1¼" x 4½", cut on crosswise grain

Blue solid
    4 strips 7½" x 76", cut on lengthwise grain

Piecing the Blocks

1 Referring to **Diagram I-A**, sew blue/green large floral 1¼" x WOF and yellow print 3" x WOF strips together to make strip set. Make 5. Press in direction of arrow. Cut into 24 segments 7" wide.

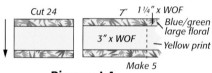

Cut 24   7"   1¼" x WOF
    Blue/green large floral
    3" x WOF
    Yellow print
    Make 5

Diagram I-A

In same manner, make strip sets and cut segments in fabric combinations and quantities shown (**Diagram I-B**).

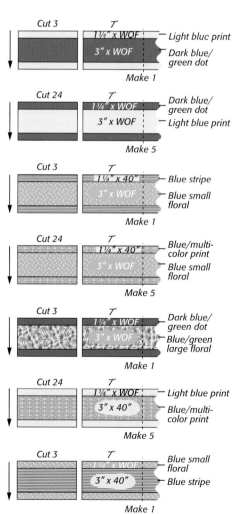

Cut 3   7"   1¼" x WOF — Light blue print
    3" x WOF — Dark blue/green dot
    Make 1

Cut 24   7"   1¼" x WOF — Dark blue/green dot
    3" x WOF — Light blue print
    Make 5

Cut 3   7"   1¼" x 40" — Blue stripe
    3" x WOF — Blue small floral
    Make 1

Cut 24   7"   1¼" x 40" — Blue/multi-color print
    3" x WOF — Blue small floral
    Make 5

Cut 3   7"   1¼" x WOF — Dark blue/green dot
    3" x WOF — Blue/green large floral
    Make 1

Cut 24   7"   1¼" x WOF — Light blue print
    3" x 40" — Blue/multi-color print
    Make 5

Cut 3   7"   1¼" x WOF — Blue small floral
    3" x 40" — Blue stripe
    Make 1

Diagram I-B

2 Stitch large floral 1¼" x 4½" strips to ends of large floral/yellow print segment to make pieced rectangle (**Diagram II-A**). Press seam allowances in direction of arrow. Make 24.

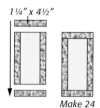

1¼" x 4½"
    Make 24

Diagram II-A

In same manner, make remaining pieced rectangles as shown (**Diagram II-B**).

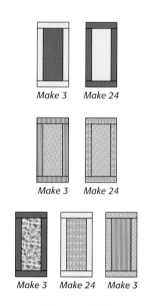

Make 3   Make 24

Make 3   Make 24

Make 3   Make 24   Make 3

Diagram II-B

3 Sew 2 horizontal rows of 3 large floral/yellow print pieced rectangles each, alternating direction of pressed seams (as shown by arrows) to make piecing easier (**Diagram III-A**). In same manner, stitch 1 row of 2 large floral/yellow print and 1 light blue print/blue green dot pieced rectangles. Sew rows together to make Open Window Block. Make 3.

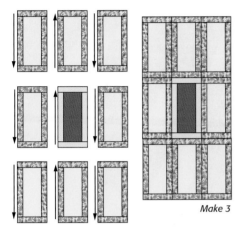

Diagram III-A

In same manner, make Open Window Blocks in fabric combinations and quantities shown in **Diagram III-B**.

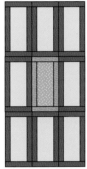

Make 3

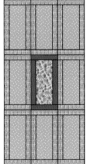

Make 3

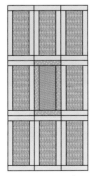

Make 3

Diagram III-B

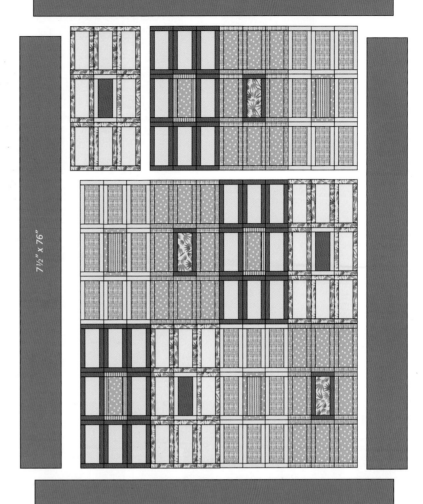

7½" x 76"

7½" x 76"

Assembly Diagram

Quilt Top Assembly
Note: Refer to **Assembly Diagram** for following step.
④ Stitch 3 rows of 4 blocks each, rotating blocks to alternate direction of pressed seams. Sew rows together. Sew blue solid 76" strips to sides; trim ends even with top and bottom. Stitch remaining blue solid strips to top/bottom; trim even with sides.

Quilting and Finishing
⑤ Layer, baste, and quilt. Julie machine quilted an allover daisy motif in the blocks, a parallel daisy and line motif in the borders, and a large daisy in each corner where the borders meet. Bind with light blue print.

Visit
McCallsQuilting.com...to check out beginner's tips for pinning as you sew. Click on Lessons, then Pinning Tips.

Designed by
HEIDI PRIDEMORE

Machine Quilted by
DORIS PRIDEMORE

Finished Quilt Size
59" x 67½"

Charm pack squares alternate

with cream rectangles in this exciting lap size
quilt. Precut fabric packs take you from shopping
directly to sewing…less cutting required!

Square-Cut Gems

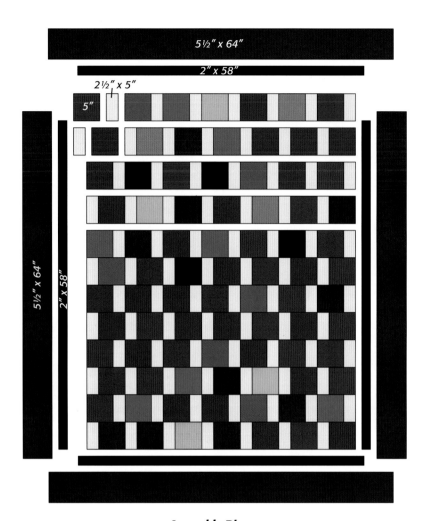

Assembly Diagram

Fabric Requirements

Assorted dark solids (piecing)	1¾-2¼ yds. **total***
Cream solid (piecing)	1 yd.
Black solid (inner border, binding)	1⅛ yds.
Burgundy solid (outer border)	1⅜ yds.
Backing (piece widthwise)	3⅞ yds.
Batting size	68" x 76"

*Or substitute two 5" charm packs of at least 42 fabric squares each; see **Planning**.

Planning

Heidi used 2 Kona® Solids Dark Palette charm packs by Robert Kaufman Fabrics for the dark squares in her dramatic throw. There are many other varieties of Kona® Solids charm packs available, so this quilt could be made in many different color schemes. Piecing is super easy…you'll have the quilt top made in no time!

Cutting Instructions
(cut in order listed)

Assorted dark solids—**cut a total of**:
   84 squares 5" x 5"
Cream solid
   84 rectangles 2½" x 5"
Black solid
   8 strips 2½" x width of fabric (WOF) for binding
   *4 strips 2" x 58", pieced from 6 WOF strips
Burgundy solid
   *4 strips 5½" x 64", pieced from 8 WOF strips

*Border strips include extra length for trimming.

Assembling the Quilt Top

Note: Refer to **Assembly Diagram** for following steps.

1 Sew 12 rows of 7 assorted squares and 7 cream rectangles each, alternating. Sew rows together, reversing direction of alternate rows.

2 Stitch black solid 58" strips to sides; trim even with top and bottom. Stitch remaining 58" strips to top/bottom; trim even with sides. Sew burgundy 64" strips to sides; trim even. Sew remaining burgundy strips to top/bottom; trim even.

Quilting and Finishing

3 Layer, baste, and quilt. Doris machine quilted leaves and looping vines in serpentine vertical rows on the dark squares. The inner border is quilted in the ditch, and the outer border features flowers and leafy vines. Bind with black solid.

Brightly colored, fast and simple to stitch, and sweet as can be…that's the recipe for a perfect play quilt!

Jelly Beans

Designed and Machine Quilted by
MICHELE SCOTT

Made by
ELINORE LOCKE

Finished Quilt Size
46″ x 58″

Number of Blocks and Finished Size
24 Letterbox Blocks
6″ x 12″

Fabric Requirements

Yellow texture, orange texture, lavender texture, green texture, **and** turquoise texture (blocks)	½ yd. **each**
Purple texture (blocks, inner border, binding)	1⅜ yds.
Multicolor mottle (outer border)	⅞ yd.
Backing (piece widthwise)	3⅛ yds.
Batting size	54″ x 66″

Planning

This quilt is divided into 4 horizontal rows of 6 blocks each. Notice that there is one block of each color arrangement in each row. You may find it helpful to use a design wall or other flat surface to position your blocks prior to assembly.

Cutting Instructions
(cut in order listed)

Yellow texture, orange texture, lavender texture, green texture, **and** turquoise texture—**cut from each:**
- 8 strips 1½" x 4½"
- 12 rectangles 2½" x 4½"
- 8 strips 1½" x 8½"
- 8 strips 2½" x 6½"

Purple texture
- 6 strips 2½" x width of fabric (WOF) for binding
- 2 strips 1½" x 52", pieced from 3 WOF strips
- 2 strips 1½" x 42", pieced from 3 WOF strips
- 8 strips 1½" x 8½"
- 8 strips 2½" x 6½"
- 8 strips 1½" x 4½"
- 12 rectangles 2½" x 4½"

Multicolor mottle
- 4 strips 4¼" x 54", pieced from 6 WOF strips

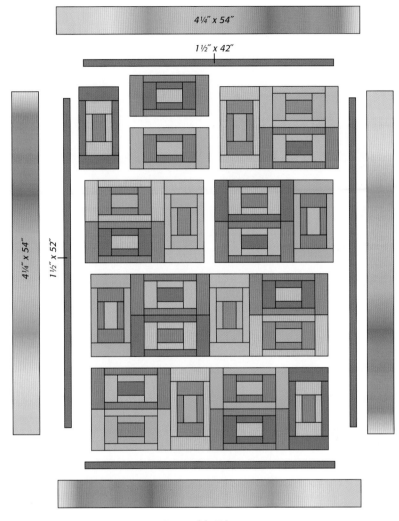

Assembly Diagram

Piecing the Blocks

1 Referring to **Diagram I**, stitch 2 yellow 1½" x 4½" strips to sides of orange 2½" x 4½" rectangle. Sew 2 yellow 2½" x 4½" rectangles to top and bottom. Stitch 2 purple 1½" x 8½" strips to sides. Sew purple 2½" x 6½" strips to top and bottom to make Letterbox Block. Make in quantities and color combinations shown.

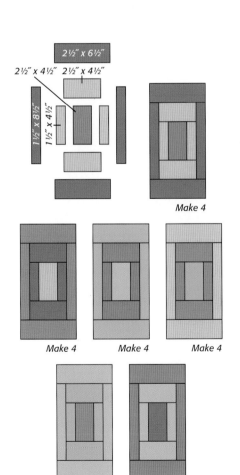

Diagram I

Quilt Top Assembly

Note: Refer to **Assembly Diagram** and photos for following steps.

2 Stitch blocks into 3-block sections, watching color placement. Make 8 total. Sew 4 rows of 2 sections each. Sew rows together.

3 Stitch purple 1½" x 52" strips to sides; trim even with top and bottom. Sew purple 42" strips to top and bottom; trim even with sides. Sew multicolor 54" strips to sides; trim even with top/bottom. Stitch remaining strips to top/bottom; trim even with sides.

Quilting and Finishing

4 Layer, baste, and quilt. Michele used Fairfield Soft Touch® batting and machine quilted an allover continuous wave and curlicue pattern. Bind with purple texture.

Designed by
GERRI ROBINSON

Machine Quilted by
REBECCA SEGURA of
Zeffie's Quilts

Finished Quilt Size
79½" x 79½"

**Number of Blocks
and Finished Sizes**
16 Small Nine-Patch
Blocks 6" x 6"
9 Large Nine-Patch
Blocks 12" x 12"

Sophia's Song

Sophisticated but soft, feminine yet
direct, today's woman is a grown-up girl who loves a
bit of luxury. Turn any corner into her cozy retreat by adding
this pretty floral throw.

Fabric Requirements

Dark pink floral (Small Nine-Patch Blocks, binding)	1¼ yds.
White/pink dot (Small Nine-Patch Blocks)	½ yd.
Assorted yellow, pink, **and** blue florals/prints (pieced rectangles)	¾-1 yd. **total each color group**
3 **each** assorted yellow, pink, **and** blue florals (Large Nine-Patch Blocks)	1 fat quarter* **each** (9 total)
Blue large floral (border)	2½ yds.
Backing	7½ yds.
Batting size	88" x 88"

*A fat quarter is an 18" x 20-22" cut of fabric.

Piecing the Blocks and Rectangles

1 Referring to **Diagram I-A**, sew together 2 dark pink floral and 1 white/pink dot WOF strips to make strip set. Make 2. Press in direction of arrows. Cut into 32 segments 2½″ wide.

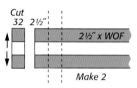

Cut
32 2½″

2½″ x WOF

Make 2

Diagram I-A

In same manner, use 2 white/pink dot and 1 dark pink WOF strips to make strip set (**Diagram I-B**). Make 1. Press, and cut into 16 segments 2½″ wide.

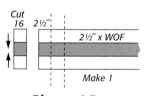

Cut
16 2½″

2½″ x WOF

Make 1

Diagram I-B

2 Sew 3 segments together to make Small Nine-Patch Block (**Diagram II**). Make 16.

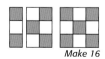

Make 16

Diagram II

Planning

To create this feminine, summery throw, Gerri included some of the Large Nine-Patch Block fabrics in her assorted pieced rectangle fabrics. Purchase additional yardage of those fabrics if you wish to do the same. Gerri also rotated some of the Large Nine-Patch Blocks for added interest. Do likewise if you wish.

Cutting Instructions
(cut in order listed)

Dark pink floral
  9 strips 2½″ x width of fabric (WOF) for binding
  5 strips 2½″ x WOF
White/pink dot
  4 strips 2½″ x WOF
Assorted yellow, pink, **and** blue florals/prints—**cut from each color group:**
  48 strips 2½″ x 6½″
3 **each** assorted yellow, pink, **and** blue florals—**cut from each:**
  9 squares 4½″ x 4½″
Blue large floral
  *2 strips 10″ x 84″, cut on lengthwise grain
  *2 strips 10″ x 64″, cut on lengthwise grain
*Border strips include extra length for trimming.

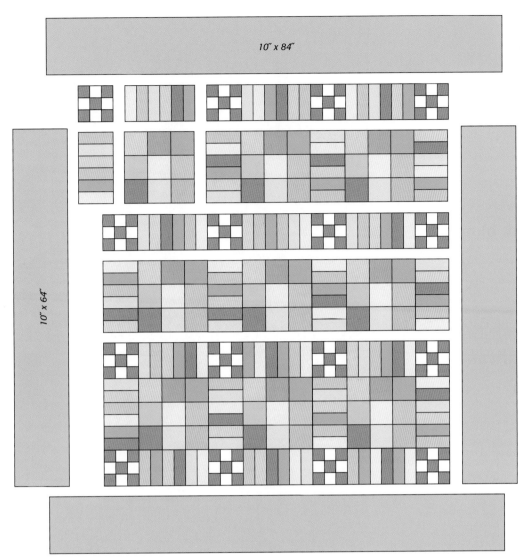

10″ x 84″

10″ x 64″

Assembly Diagram

③ Referring to **Diagram III**, stitch together 2 each assorted yellow, pink, and blue 2½″ x 6½″ strips to make pieced rectangle. Make 24 total.

2½″ x 6½″

Make 24 total

Diagram III

④ Stitch together nine 4½″ squares (1 of each fabric) to make Large Nine-Patch Block (**Diagram IV**). Make 9.

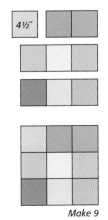

4½″

Make 9

Diagram IV

Assembling the Quilt Top

Note: Refer to **Assembly Diagram** for following steps.

⑤ Sew 4 narrow rows using 4 Small Nine-Patch Blocks and 3 pieced rectangles each. Stitch 3 wide rows using 4 pieced rectangles and 3 Large Nine-Patch Blocks each. Sew rows together, alternating.

⑥ Sew blue large floral 64″ strips to sides; trim even with top and bottom. Stitch remaining blue large floral strips to top/bottom; trim even with sides.

Quilting and Finishing

⑦ Layer, baste, and quilt. Rebecca machine quilted a large allover feather design. Bind with dark pink floral.

Red, white, & blue fabrics from your stash create easy pieced blocks for this patriotic bed size quilt. Add coordinating sashing, border, and binding fabrics, and you're ready for an **all-American nap!**

Hometown Afternoon

Designed by
SARAH MAXWELL
and DOLORES SMITH

Machine Quilted by
CONNIE GRESHAM

Finished Quilt Size 75½" x 90⅝"

Number of Blocks and Finished Size
20 Pieced Blocks 12⅛" x 12⅛"

Fabric Requirements

White/red print (block backgrounds)	1⅜ yds.
Assorted blue prints (blocks)	1⅝-2 yds. **total**
Assorted red prints (blocks)	1⅛-1½ yds. **total**
Light blue/white print (sashing posts)	½ yd.
Red/white stripe (sashing)	1⅞ yds.
Light blue/white/red large print (border)	1¾ yds.
Medium blue/white print (binding)	1 yd.
Backing (piece widthwise)	7⅛ yds.
Batting size	84" x 100"

Planning

Quick and fun, this scrappy, sparkly quilt is a great stash-buster. Have fun exploring your stash to come up with your favorite fabric combinations.

Cutting Instructions

⊠ = cut in half twice diagonally
◻ = cut in half diagonally
White/red print
    40 squares 5⅜" x 5⅜" ⊠
    40 squares 3" x 3" ◻
Assorted blue prints—**cut 40 sets of:**
    4 matching squares 3⅜" x 3⅜"
Assorted red prints—**cut 20 sets of:**
    5 matching squares 3⅜" x 3⅜"
Light blue/white print
    30 squares 3½" x 3½"
Red/white stripe
    49 strips 3½" x 12⅝"
Light blue/white/red large print
    4 strips 6¼" x 84", pieced from 9 width
       of fabric (WOF) strips
Medium blue/white print
    10 strips 2½" x WOF (binding)

Piecing the Blocks

1 Referring to **Diagram I**, stitch 2 white/red print 5⅜" quarter-square triangles to sides of assorted blue 3⅜" square. Add white/red 3" half-square triangle to make pieced triangle. Make 20 sets of 4 matching.

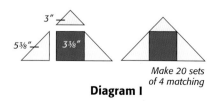

Diagram I

2 Using 5 matching red 3⅜" squares and 4 matching blue 3⅜" squares, sew 3 rows (**Diagram II**). Stitch rows together to make nine-patch. Make 20 total.

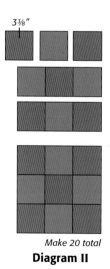

Make 20 total
Diagram II

3 Referring to **Diagram III**, stitch 4 matching pieced triangles to sides of nine-patch to make Pieced Block. **Trim** block to 12⅝" square if needed. Make 20 total.

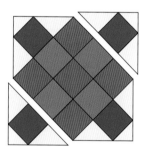

Make 20 total
Diagram III

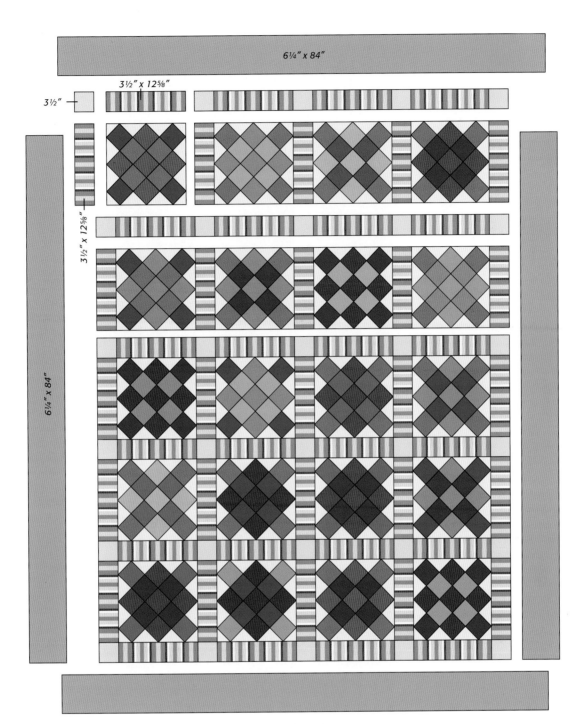

Assembly Diagram

Quilt Top Assembly

Note: Refer to **photos** and **Assembly Diagram** for following steps.

4 Sew together 5 light blue/white print 3½" squares and 4 red/white stripe 12⅝" strips to make sashing strip. Make 6. Stitch together 5 red/white stripe strips and 4 blocks to make block row. Make 5 total. Sew sashing strips and block rows together, alternating.

5 Sew light blue/white/red large print 84" strips to sides; trim even with top and bottom. Sew light blue/white/red strips to top/bottom; trim even with sides.

Quilting and Finishing

6 Layer, baste, and quilt. Connie machine quilted an 8-petaled motif in the blocks, quatrefoils in the sashing posts, and a stem and leaf design in the sashing. The border is filled with bat and baseball shapes. Bind with medium blue/white print.

Designed
by BEVERLY
SULLIVANT

Machine Quilted
by BARBARA SHIE

Finished Quilt Size
46″ x 71½″ [54½″ x 71½″]

Number of Blocks and Finished Size
40 [48] Framed Square Blocks 8½″ x 8½″

Made with Love

The members of Reverend Beverly Sullivant's congregation in Montclair Heights, New Jersey, are blessed with her devotion not only as a pastor, but also as a generous and thoughtful quilter. When someone needs comfort, Beverly is often there with one of her unique Caring Quilts, made using novelty fabrics that reflect the interests and life history of its recipient.

Beverly created 2 sample quilts for us, based on fictional recipients and their stories. The smaller (pink sashing) quilt was made for a woman who grew up on a farm, became a teacher, and loves cats. She is a breast cancer survivor, and plans to visit Paris and Hawaii to celebrate her continuing good health. The larger (black sashing) quilt on page 48 was made for a man, a former Marine, who likes New York City, long road trips, music, and games of chance. He and his grandson love to go to baseball games and always treat themselves to hot pretzels at the stadium.

To make your own version of Beverly's design, select novelty prints that depict objects and places that the quilt's recipient will enjoy. Any directional fabrics used for the block center squares are oriented randomly, so that there are prints to enjoy from any angle. Instructions are for the smaller quilt; where they differ from the smaller quilt, instructions for the larger quilt are given [in brackets].

Caring Quilts

Novelty fabrics unified by simple sashing make this easy design perfect for gift-giving. Start one today as a spirit lifter for a special somebody.

Fabric Requirements

Assorted novelty prints
(blocks) 3¼–3¾ yds.
total
[3¾–4¼ yds.
total]

Pink print [black solid]
(sashing, binding) 1⅛ yds.
Backing (piece
widthwise) 3⅛ yds.
[3⅝ yds.]
Batting size 54" x 80"
[64" x 82"]

Cutting Instructions

Assorted novelty prints
cut 40 [48] matching sets of:
2 strips 2" x 6"
2 strips 2" x 9"
cut a total of:
40 [48] squares 6" x 6"
Pink print [black solid]
*7 strips 2½" x width of fabric (WOF)
for binding
*2 strips 2" x 50" [2" x 58"], pieced from
3 WOF strips
2 strips 2" x 51½", pieced from 3 WOF
strips
4 strips 2" x 9"
*Cut first

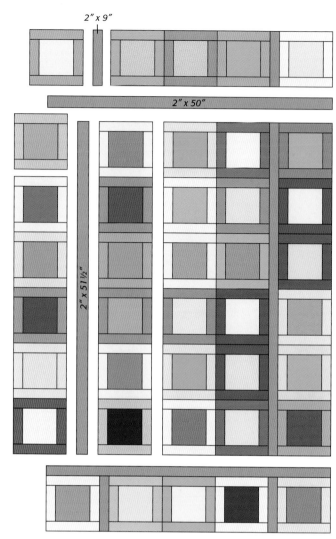

Smaller Quilt Assembly Diagram

Piecing the Quilt Top

① Sew matching 6" strips to sides of assorted 6" square (**Diagram I**). Sew matching 9" strips to top and bottom to make Framed Square Block. Make 40 [48] total.

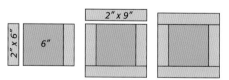

*Make 40 total
[48 for larger quilt]*
Diagram I

② **Note:** Refer to **Smaller Quilt [Larger Quilt] Assembly Diagram** for following steps. Stitch 5 [6] vertical block rows using 6 blocks each. Sew together block rows and pink [black] 51½" strips in order shown to make quilt center.

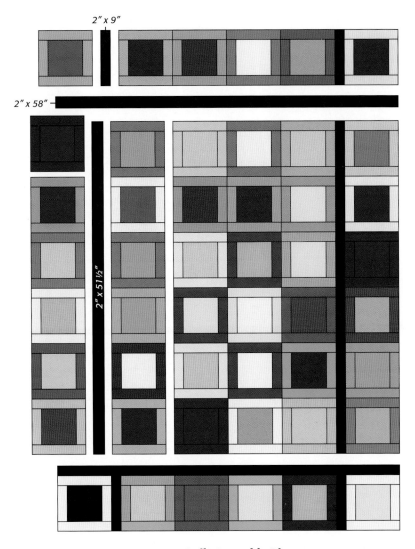

2" x 9"

2" x 58"

2" x 51½"

Larger Quilt Assembly Diagram

3 Sew top and bottom block rows using 5 [6] blocks and 2 pink [black] 9″ strips each.

4 Stitch together top and bottom block rows, 2 pink 50″ [black 58″] sashing strips, and quilt center in order shown, trimming sashing strips even with blocks after each addition.

Quilting and Finishing

5 Layer, baste, and quilt. Barbara machine quilted meandering heart designs. Bind with pink print [black solid].

Color Notes

When combining lots of scrappy blocks, a single sashing/binding fabric can unify the quilt. Select fabric in one of your quilt recipient's favorite colors, as a solid or textural print, to tie your Caring Quilt together.

Designed by
SHERRI BAIN DRIVER

Need a fast, fun quilt for someone special? Our photos show you how to use free-motion stitching to **appliqué raw-edge "tags"** and machine quilt, all at the same time!

Rag Tag Cuddler

Finished Quilt Size
42½″ x 54½″

Number of Blocks and Finished Size
24 A Blocks 6″ x 9″
18 B Blocks 6″ x 9″

Fabric Requirements
Assorted yellow prints, lime prints, **and** aqua prints (blocks)	⅞-1¼ yds. **total** each color group
*Assorted bright prints (appliqué "tags")	⅞-1¼ yds. **total**
Aqua stripe (binding)	⅝ yd.
Backing (piece widthwise)	2⅞ yds.
Batting size	50″ x 62″

*See **Planning**.

Planning

If you save small fabric scraps, here's a fun way to use them in a super-easy quilt. You'll piece a simple top, and then layer and baste it for machine quilting. Before starting to quilt, you'll place scrap "tags" on your quilt sandwich and stitch them in place as you machine quilt. This is a great way to learn (or practice) free-motion quilting...our photos get you started! The tags can be any size (on the featured quilt, they range from 1⅜" x 2" to 4" x 4½"). Most are square or rectangular, but a few are slightly irregular. Tags can be any color you want, but they'll show up best if they contrast with the background blocks. You may want to select fabrics for tags and cut shapes as you go when you reach Step 3.

Cutting Instructions

Assorted yellow prints, lime prints, **and aqua prints—cut from each color group:**
   42 rectangles 3½" x 6½"
Assorted bright prints
   100-175 squares/rectangles
      (See **Planning** and Step 3)
Aqua stripe
   6 strips 2½" x width of fabric
      (binding)

Piecing the Blocks

① Referring to **Diagram I**, sew together 1 each yellow, lime, and aqua rectangles to make A Block. Make 24 total.

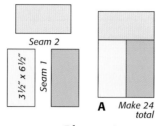

Seam 2

3½" x 6½"

Seam 1

A   *Make 24 total*

Diagram I

Make 18 total B Blocks in arrangement shown in **Diagram II**.

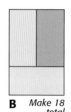

B   *Make 18 total*

Diagram II

Assembling the Quilt Top

② Refer to **Assembly Diagram** for this step. Sew 4 vertical rows of 6 A Blocks each. Stitch 3 vertical rows of 6 B Blocks each. Sew rows together, alternating.

Assembly Diagram

Free-Motion Quilting Fun

Free-motion quilting allows you to quilt in any direction (forward, backward, side-to-side, diagonally...you can even quilt your name in cursive!) without rotating your quilt sandwich. To set up your machine for this, attach a darning foot or free-motion foot, and lower the feed dogs (consult your owner's manual for details, if necessary).

Insert a new needle (jeans/denim 12 is versatile) and thread the top of the machine and bobbin with a high-quality thread. An accessory to extend the bed of your machine is very helpful to support the quilt. You may find finger cots or quilters' gloves handy for gripping your project as you quilt. When free-motion quilting, your hands guide the quilt under the needle, controlling the direction and size of the stitches. To make smaller stitches, move your hands more slowly, and/or run the machine faster. For larger stitches, move your hands faster and/or run the machine more slowly. Have fun with this project and don't worry if your stitching is wiggly and uneven...it's a whimsical quilt, and keep in mind that tag edges will curl and cover some quilting when you launder the quilt.

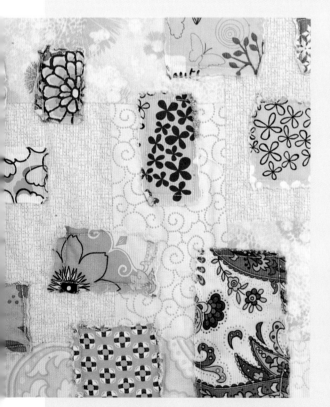

Quilting and Finishing

Note: See **Free-Motion Quilting Fun** (page 52) for help with this step. Contrasting thread was used in photos for clarity.

③ Layer and pin-baste backing, batting, and quilt top for machine quilting (**photo A**).

Starting near center, arrange approximately 20 tags on sandwiched quilt top as desired, centered on patches or extending across seams (**photo B**).

Pin tags in place, pinning through all layers, and being sure to remove any safety pins from under the tags (**photo C**).

Beginning inside the edge of a tag, take one stitch. With the needle up, gently pull on the top thread to bring a loop of bobbin thread to the surface (**photo D**).

Pull the loop until the end of the bobbin thread comes up. Holding both threads taut and out of the way, make several tiny stitches to secure the stitching line. Sew around the first tag, about ¼″ from raw edges (**photo E**).

When you return to the starting point, stitch across the background to an adjacent tag. Stitch around the 2nd tag (**photo F**), and when completed, stitch to another.

Continue in this manner, quilting over previous stitching as necessary to reach adjacent tags (**photos G, H,** and **I**). When tags in this section are all secured, pin more tags in place, and stitch as before. To securely end a stitching line, make several tiny stitches. Trim beginning and ending threads close to quilt surface, or bury thread tails in batting layer of quilt using a large-eyed needle.

④ Bind with aqua stripe. Machine wash and dry to fluff edges of tags, cleaning lint trap often.

Visit
McCallsQuilting.com…
for help with every part of the binding process. Click on **Lessons**, then **Binding**.

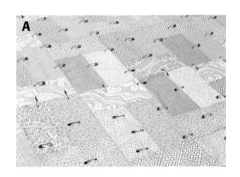

A

D

G

B

E

H

C

F

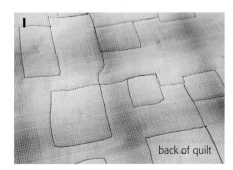

I

back of quilt

Semper Fi

Designed by
JULIE TANNEHILL

Finished Quilt Size
57" x 85¼"

**Number of Blocks
and Finished Size**
34 Rail Fence Blocks
10" x 10"

A Hero's Comfort

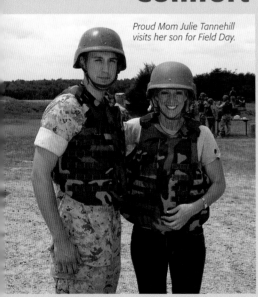

Proud Mom Julie Tannehill visits her son for Field Day.

"My son thinks I can do anything, and I admit my ego often causes me to rise to the occasion. I would not want to disappoint him! Over the years I have heard "...my mom can do that…" and I give it my best shot. Sometimes it even works out!

When he was leaving for his first deployment as a Marine Corps Officer (not such a fun Mom moment) he shipped 2 of his uniforms to me and asked for a quilt to take with him. Both surprised and touched, I set about figuring it out. My quilting friends had a hand in all of this planning, as it of course had to be just right. After several "have you considered this?" discussions, I settled on a pattern idea.

My husband cut as many 10½" squares and 2½" strips as possible out of 1 old and 1 new uniform that didn't fit. Quilters know about the straight of grain, but let me just say, garments are a challenge to keep with the grain line!

Creating and sewing this quilt was challenging and soothing at the same time.

Realizing that the willingness of those who serve this country is what makes it so easy for us to enjoy our hobbies in peace and security is an overwhelming thought. More than ever I appreciate the freedom protected by those who will tell us they are simply doing their job. A quilt is a small way to express that thankfulness as well as a way for one mom to feel like she could wrap her son in love while away."

Julie's extra-long twin quilt is perfect to cover a bunk or berth. Some of the patches are cut off the straight of grain and include pocket, button, and seam details, adding dimension and interest. Julie included a tan texture and black solid to complete the top and binding, and backed the quilt with a Marine Corps print.

This quilt has seen a lot of active duty, deploying along with its owner. No matter how far he is from home, his mother's love and caring go with this Marine, along with her unique quilt design.

For any service person on active duty, a quilt from home means comfort and caring, and is a tangible **reminder that loved ones are awaiting their safe return.** This simple design is easy to piece, and lends itself well to any favorite fabric theme or color scheme.

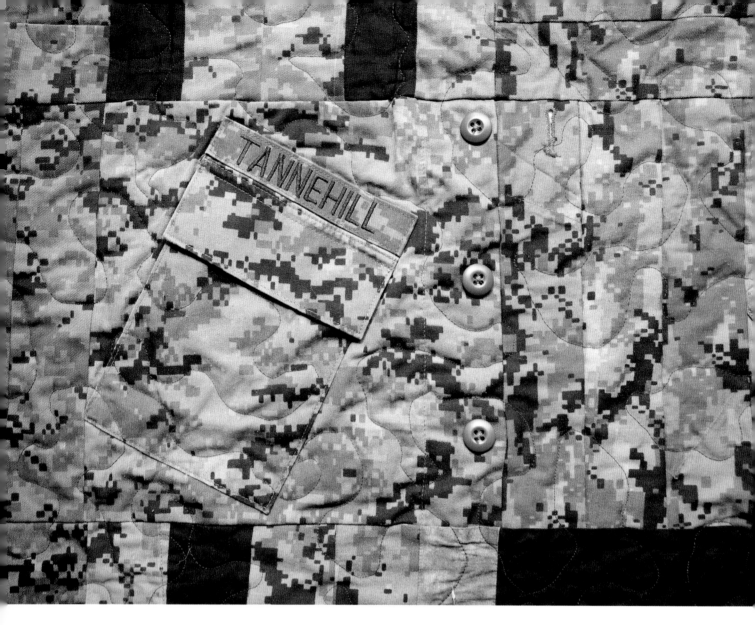

Fabric Requirements

Tan texture (blocks)	7/8 yd.
Camouflage print (blocks, squares)	3 3/8 yds.
Black solid (blocks, setting triangles, binding)	2 3/4 yds.
Backing (piece lengthwise)	5 3/8 yds.
Batting size	66" x 94"

Cutting Instructions

⊠ = cut in half twice diagonally

◺ = cut in half diagonally

Tan texture
   28 strips 2½" x 10½"
Camouflage print
   *5 squares 10½" x 10½"
   114 strips 2½" x 10½"
Black solid
   *8 strips 2½" x width of fabric
      (binding)
   *4 squares 17" x 17" ⊠
   *2 squares 9" x 9" ◺
   28 strips 2½" x 10½"
*Cut first.

Piecing the Quilt Top

❶ Referring to **Diagram I**, sew 5 tan/camouflage/black 2½" x 10½" strips together in random order to make Rail Fence Block. Make 34 total.

Make 34 total

Diagram I

9″

17″

10½″

Assembly Diagram

2 Note: Refer to **Assembly Diagram** for this step. The setting triangles on all edges and corners are cut oversized to allow trimming quilt edges even after assembly. Sew 9 diagonal rows using black 17″ quarter-square triangles, blocks, and camouflage print 10½″ squares. Sew rows together. Stitch black 9″ half-square triangles to corners. **Trim** edges even.

Quilting and Finishing
3 Layer, baste, and quilt. Julie machine quilted a large meander in black thread. Bind with black solid.

Artful Simplicity

Designed by
KARI NICHOLS

Machine Quilted by
PAM COSGROVE

Finished Quilt Size
61½″ x 75½″

Whether you're a first-time quilter or a seasoned hand, this design is a fast, fun way to show off beautiful fabrics. Strip-piecing a few segments is the only construction step before assembling the quilt top.

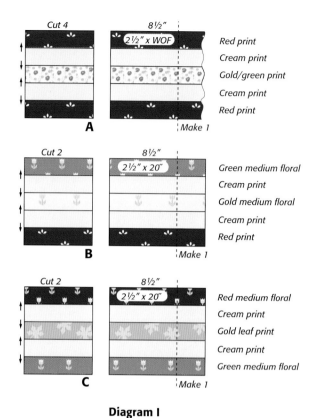

Red print
Cream print
Gold/green print
Cream print
Red print

Cut 4 / 8½" / 2½" x WOF / **A** / Make 1

Green medium floral
Cream print
Gold medium floral
Cream print
Red print

Cut 2 / 8½" / 2½" x 20" / **B** / Make 1

Red medium floral
Cream print
Gold leaf print
Cream print
Green medium floral

Cut 2 / 8½" / 2½" x 20" / **C** / Make 1

Diagram I

Fabric Requirements

Red print (piecing, binding)	1 yd.
Cream print (piecing, inner border)	1⅝ yds.
Gold/green print, green medium floral, gold medium floral, red medium floral, **and** gold leaf print (piecing)	⅛ yd. **each**
Red large floral (center panel)	¾ yd.*
Green leaf print (side panels)	¾ yd.
Red/gold medium floral (outer border)	2⅛ yds.
Backing (piece lengthwise)	4⅞ yds.
Batting size	70" x 84"

*Based on 40½" of usable width.

A Beginners Bouquet

Kari created the perfect showcase for beautiful floral coordinates. The simple strip piecing makes it a great first quilt for a beginner, or a quick project for the more advanced quilter.

Cutting Instructions
(cut in order listed)

Red print
  8 strips 2½" x width of fabric (WOF) for binding
  2 strips 2½" x WOF
  1 strip 2½" x 20"

Cream print
  4 strips 2½" x 64" pieced from 8 WOF strips
  2 strips 2½" x 54" pieced from 3 WOF strips
  2 strips 2½" x WOF
  4 strips 2½" x 20"
  2 strips 2½" x 22½"
  8 strips 2½" x 10½"
  2 strips 2½" x 8½"

Gold/green print
  1 strip 2½" x WOF

Green medium floral
  2 strips 2½" x 20

Gold medium floral, red medium floral, **and** gold leaf print—**cut from each:**
  1 strip 2½" x 20"

Red large floral
  1 rectangle 22½" x 40½"

Green leaf print
  2 strips 10½" x 36½"

Red/gold medium floral
  4 strips 6" x 68", cut on lengthwise grain

Piecing the Segments

❶ Sew together 2 red print, 2 cream print, and 1 gold/green print WOF strips in order shown (**Diagram I**). Make 1. Press seams in direction of arrows. Cut into four A segments 8½" wide. Sew together 1 green medium floral, 2 cream print, 1 gold medium floral, and 1 red print 20" strips. Make 1. Press, and cut two B segments 8½" wide. In same manner, make remaining strip set and cut two C segments as shown.

Quilt Top Assembly

Note: Refer to **Assembly Diagram** for following steps.

❷ To make side panel, sew together 4 cream print 10½" strips, two A segments, and 1 green leaf print 36½" strip. Make 2.

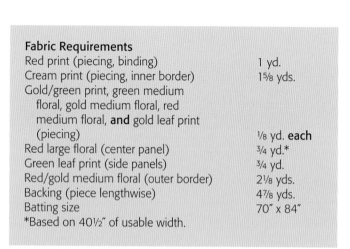

Visit
McCallsQuilting.com

Visit our website for a pattern for a coordinating table runner.

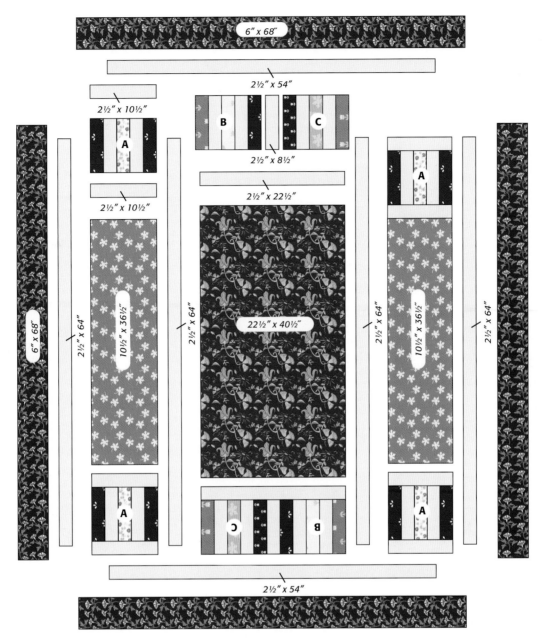

Assembly Diagram

Within the diagram:
- 6" x 68"
- 2½" x 54"
- 2½" x 10½"
- B
- C
- 2½" x 8½"
- 2½" x 22½"
- A
- 2½" x 10½"
- A
- 6" x 68"
- 2½" x 64"
- 10½" x 36½"
- 2½" x 64"
- 22½" x 40½"
- 2½" x 64"
- 10½" x 36½"
- 2½" x 64"
- A
- C
- B
- A
- 2½" x 54"
- 2½" x 54"

③ Stitch together 1 segment B, 1 cream 8½" strip, and 1 segment C to make center panel top/bottom strip. Make 2. Join center panel top/bottom strips, 2 cream 22½" strips, and red large floral 40½" rectangle to make center panel.

④ Sew together 2 side panels, 2 cream 64" strips, and center panel, **trimming** cream strips even with panels after each addition.

⑤ Stitch cream 64" strips to sides; trim even with top/bottom. Stitch cream 54" strips to top/bottom; trim even with sides. Sew red/gold medium floral 68" strips to sides; trim even. Sew remaining red/gold 68" strips to top/bottom; trim even.

Quilting and Finishing
⑥ Layer, baste, and quilt. Pam machine quilted an allover large floral pattern. Bind with red print. For help with binding, visit **McCallsQuilting.com** and click on Lessons, then Binding.

Color Notes

When showcasing large prints in a panel, consider using high contrast fabrics. The red large floral in this quilt shows nicely against the light cream background. In addition, Kari chose colors that are complementary on the color wheel (opposite each other) in the red and green panels.

Basic Quiltmaking Instructions

These instructions offer a brief introduction to quiltmaking. Quiltmaking instructions for projects in this issue are written for the individual with some sewing experience. Review this information if you are making your first quilt.

All fabric requirements are based on 40"/42"-wide fabric.

The yardage given includes an additional 5% to account for fabric shrinkage and individual differences in cutting.

A ¼" seam allowance is included on pattern pieces when required.

All measurements for pieces, sashing, and borders include ¼" seam allowances.

The finished quilt size is the size of the quilt before quilting.

Because each quiltmaker usually has a personal preference, the type of batting to be used for each quilt will not be listed, unless it is necessary to obtain a specific look.

SUPPLIES
Scissors (for paper and template plastic)
Iron and ironing board
Marking tools: pencils, chalk markers, fine-point permanent marker (such as Pilot or Sharpie®)
Needles: package of sharps (for hand piecing) assorted sizes; package of betweens (for hand quilting), size Nos. 8 to 12
Quilting hoop or frame
Pins and pincushion
Rotary cutter and mat (at least 18" x 24")
Rulers: 2" x 18"; clear acrylic 12" square; clear acrylic 6" x 24" (for use with a rotary cutter)
Sewing machine (for machine piecing)
Shears, 8" (for fabric)
Template plastic
Thimble to fit the middle finger of your sewing hand
Thread: cotton thread or monofilament, size .004 (for machine quilting); quilting thread (for hand quilting); sewing thread in colors to match your fabrics

FABRIC PREPARATION
Pre-wash fabric to remove excess dye and minimize shrinking of completed project. Machine wash gently in warm water, dry on warm setting, and press. Immerse a swatch of fabric in a clear glass of water to test colorfastness; if dye appears, soak fabric in equal parts of white vinegar and water. Rinse and dry fabric; test another swatch. If dye still appears, do not use the fabric.

PRESSING
Proper pressing is a prerequisite for accurate piecing. Press with a light touch, using iron tip and an up and down movement. Save continuous motion "ironing" for wrinkled fabric. Use either steam or dry heat, whichever works best, and assembly-type pressing to save time.

Choose a pressing plan before beginning a project and stay consistent, if possible. Seams are "set" by first being pressed flat and then pressed either to one side, usually toward the darker fabric, or open. Sometimes, both are used in the same project, depending on the design.

To prevent distortion, press long, sewn strips widthwise and avoid raw bias edges. Other pressing hints are: use distilled water, avoid a too-hot iron which will cause fabric shininess, and pre-treat wrinkled or limp fabric with a liberal amount of spray fabric sizing.

TEMPLATES
Make templates by placing transparent plastic over the printed template pattern and tracing with a fine-point permanent marker. Trace and cut out on the stitching line (broken line) for hand-piecing templates; cut on the outer solid line for machine-piecing templates.

Label each template with the name of the quilt, template letter, grain line, and match points (dots) where sewing lines intersect. Pierce a small hole at each match point for marking match points on fabric.

FABRIC MARKING & CUTTING
Position fabric wrong side up, and place the template on the fabric. With a marker or well-sharpened pencil, trace around the template and mark match points. For hand-piecing templates, allow enough space for ¼" seam allowances to be added. For machine-piecing templates, cut along the drawn line. For hand-piecing, cut ¼" beyond the drawn line.

PIECING
Stitch fabric pieces together for patchwork by hand or machine.

Hand Piecing
Place two fabric pieces right sides together. With point of pin, match corner or other match points to align seamlines; pin. Use about an 18"-long single strand of quality sewing thread and sewing needle of your choice. To secure thread, begin at a match point and, without a knot, take a stitch and a backstitch on the seamline. Make smooth running stitches, closely and evenly spaced, stitching on the drawn line on both patches of fabric. Backstitch at the end of the seam-

How to Make Continuous Bias

1 Measure the quilt to determine how many inches of binding you need. Allow 10" extra for turning corners and the closure. Refer to chart to find the size square needed.

2 Cut the square in half diagonally (see **Diagrams A-C**). With right sides together, sew the triangles together with a ¼" seam and press open.

3 On fabric wrong side long edges, draw lines to make strips of your chosen binding width (see **Diagram D**). Use a clear acrylic rotary ruler and a pencil or fine-point permanent pen to draw the lines.

4 Bring the short diagonal edges together (see **Diagrams E** and **F**), forming a tube. Offset the drawn lines by one strip. With right sides together, match lines with pins at the ¼" seamline and stitch seam; press open.

5 With scissors, cut along continuously drawn line (see **Diagram G**).

line. Do not stitch into the seam allowances. Press seams after the block is completed.

To join seamed pieces and strengthen the intersection, stitch through the seam allowances, and backstitch directly before and immediately after them.

Machine Piecing

Use a ¼"-wide presser foot for a seaming guide, or place a strip of opaque tape on the machine throat plate ¼" from the needle position. Place 2 fabric pieces right sides together, raw edges aligned, and pin perpendicular to the future seamline to secure. Begin and end stitching at the raw edges without backstitching; do not sew over pins. Make sure the thread tension and stitches are smooth and even on both sides of the seam. When joining seamed pieces, butt or match seams, pin to secure, and stitch. Press each seam before continuing to the next.

To chain-piece, repeatedly feed pairs of fabric pieces under the presser foot while taking a few stitches without any fabric under the needle between pairs. Cut the chained pieces apart before or after pressing.

APPLIQUÉING
Hand Appliqué

Needle-Turn Method. Place the template on the fabric right side. Draw around the template with a non-permanent marking tool of your choice, making a line no darker than necessary to be visible. Cut out the shape, including a scant ¼" seam allowance on all sides. Experience makes "eye-balling" the seam allowance quick and easy.

To blind stitch the appliqué shapes, position the appliqué shape on the background fabric, securing with a pin or a dab of glue stick. Select a sewing thread color to match the appliqué fabric. A 100% cotton thread is less visible than a cotton/polyester blend.

Begin stitching on a straight or gently curved edge, not at a sharp point or corner. Turn under a short length of seam allowance using your fingers and the point of your needle. Insert the needle into the seamline of the appliqué piece, coming up from the wrong side and catching just one or two threads on the edge. Push the needle through the background fabric exactly opposite the point where the thread was stitched onto the appliqué fabric piece. Coming up from the wrong side, take a stitch through the background fabric and appliqué piece, again catching just a couple threads of the appliqué fabric. Allow about ⅛" between stitches. The thread is visible on the wrong side of your block and almost invisible on the right side.

As you stitch around the edge of an appliqué fabric piece, turn under the seam allowance as you work, following the drawn line on the right side of the fabric, using your fingers and the point of the needle.

Freezer Paper Method I. Trace the template shape onto the dull side of freezer paper and cut out. With a dry iron, press the freezer paper shape, shiny side down, onto the applique fabric right side. Cut out the fabric, including a scant ¼" seam allowance on all sides. To stitch, follow the same procedure used in the Needle-Turn Method. Rather than using the drawn line as your guide, use the edge of the freezer paper.

Freezer Paper Method II. Trace the template shape onto the dull side of freezer paper and cut out. With a dry iron, press the freezer paper shape, shiny side down, onto the appliqué fabric wrong side. Cut out the fabric, including a scant ¼" seam allowance on all sides. Finger-press the seam allowance to the back of the paper template and baste in place. To stitch an appliqué fabric piece, follow the same procedure used in the Needle-Turn Method. The seam allowance has already been turned under in this technique. To remove the freezer paper, shortly before closing the appliqué, remove the basting and pluck out the freezer paper with a tweezers; or after the appliqué is sewn, cut the background fabric away behind the appliqué and remove the paper.

To reverse appliqué, two fabric pieces are layered on the background fabric, the edges of the top fabric are cut in a particular design and turned under to reveal the underlying fabric. Pin or glue the bottom appliqué fabric into position on the background block. Cut the top fabric along the specified cutting lines. Place the top fabric over the bottom fabric; check the position of the bottom fabric by holding the block up to a light source and pin. Use the Needle-Turn Method to turn under the top fabric seam allowance and appliqué, and to reveal the fabric underneath.

Machine Appliqué

Trace templates without seam allowances on paper side of paper-backed fusible web. Cut out, leaving a small margin beyond the drawn lines. Following manufacturer's instructions, apply to wrong side of appliqué fabric. Cut out on drawn line. Position appliqué on quilt where desired, and fuse to quilt following manufacturer's instructions. Finish appliqué edges by machine using a buttonhole stitch, satin stitch, or stitch of your choice.

MITERING CORNERS

Miter border corners when an angled seam complements the overall design of the quilt. Cut border strips the finished length and width of the quilt plus 4"-6" extra.

Center and pin border strips in place. Start and end seams ¼" from raw edges; backstitch to secure. Press seams away from quilt center. Lay quilt top right side up on ironing board and fold each border end flat back onto itself, right sides together, forming a 45° angle at the quilt's corner. Press to form sharp creases. Fold quilt on diagonal, right sides together. Align border strip raw edges, border seams at the ¼" backstitched point, and creases; pin in place. Stitch along crease, backstitching at ¼" border seam. Press seam open. With quilt right side up, align 45°-angle line of square ruler on seamline to check accuracy. If corner is flat and square, trim excess fabric to ¼" seam allowance.

For multiple mitered borders, sew strips together first and attach to quilt as one unit.

MARKING QUILTING PATTERNS

Press quilt top and change any correctable irregularities. Choose a marking

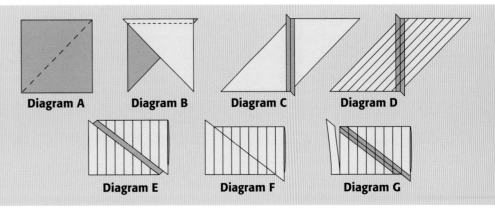

SIZE SQUARE TO CUT			
Length Needed	2"-Wide Bias Strip	2½"-Wide Bias Strip	3"-Wide Bias Strip
110"	16" square	18" square	20" square
220"	23" square	26" square	28" square
340"	28" square	32" square	35" square
480"	33" square	37" square	40" square

Diagram A Diagram B Diagram C Diagram D

Diagram E Diagram F Diagram G

tool which makes a thin accurate line, and pre-test removability on quilt fabric scraps.

Marking tool options include: water-soluble and air-erasable markers, white dressmaker's pencil, chalk pencils, chalk rolling markers, and slivers of hardened soap. Try silver and yellow Berol® pencils on dark fabrics and a No. 2 pencil sparingly on light fabric. The same project may need several types of markers.

Design aid options include: freezer-paper cutouts, stencils, templates, household items such as cookie cutters, and acrylic rulers.

After marking quilting designs of choice, do not press quilt top; markings could be set permanently.

BACKING

Use the same quality backing fabric as used in the quilt top. Remove selvages and cut backing at least 4" larger than quilt top on all sides. It is necessary to seam backing for quilts larger than 36" wide when using standard 44"/45"-wide fabric. Use either vertical or horizontal seaming, whichever requires less fabric. Press backing seams open.

BATTING

Standard pre-cut batting sizes are:

Crib	45" x 60"
Twin	72" x 90"
Double	81" x 96"
Queen	90" x 108"
King	120" x 120"

Consider several factors when choosing batting. How do you want the quilt to look? How close will the quilting stitches be? Are you hand or machine quilting? How will the quilt be used?

Batting is made from different fibers (not all fibers are available in all sizes). If you prefer an old-fashioned looking quilt, consider using a mostly cotton batting. The newer cotton battings are bonded and do not require the close quilting that old-fashioned cotton battings once did. If you don't want to do a lot of quilting, use a regular or low-loft polyester batting. If you like "puffy" quilts, use a high-loft polyester batting. Wool battings are also available.

If you are not sure which batting is right for your project, consult the professionals at your local quilt shop.

LAYERING THE QUILT SANDWICH

Mark the center of the backing on the wrong side at the top, bottom, and side edges. On a smooth, flat surface a little larger than the quilt, place backing right side down. Smooth any wrinkles until the backing is flat; use masking tape to hold it taut and in place.

Unfold batting and lay over backing. Smooth wrinkles, keeping the backing wrinkle free.

Position quilt top on backing and batting, keeping all layers wrinkle free. Match centers of quilt top with backing. Use straight pins to keep layers from shifting while basting.

BASTING

Basting holds the three layers together to prevent shifting while quilting.

For hand quilting, baste using a long needle threaded with as long a length of sewing thread as can be used without tangling. Insert needle through all layers in center of quilt and baste layers together with a long running stitch. For the first line of basting, stitch up and down the vertical center of the quilt. Next, baste across the horizontal center of the quilt. Working toward the edges and creating a grid, continue basting to completely stabilize the layers.

For machine quilting, pin-baste using nickel-plated safety pins, instead of needle and thread. Begin in the center of the quilt and work outward to the edges, placing safety pins approximately every 4".

QUILTING
Hand Quilting

Hand quilting features evenly spaced, small stitches on both sides of the quilt with no knots showing on the back.

Most quilters favor 100% cotton thread in ecru or white, though beautiful colors are available.

Beginners start with a size 8 or 9 "between" needle and advance to a shorter, finer size 10 or 12 needle for finer stitching. Use a well-fitting, puncture-proof thimble on the middle finger of your sewing hand to position and push the needle through the quilt layers.

A frame or hoop keeps the layered quilt smooth and taut; choose from a variety of shapes and sizes. Select a comfortable seat with proper back support and a good light source, preferably natural light, to reduce eye strain.

To begin, cut thread 24" long and make a knot on one end. Place the needle tip either into a seamline or ½" behind the point where quilting stitches are to begin and guide it through the batting and up through the quilt top to "bury" the knot. Gently pull on the thread until you hear the knot "pop" through the quilt top. Trim the thread tail.

To quilt using a running stitch, hold the needle parallel to the quilt top and stitch up and down through the three layers with a rocking motion, making several stitches at a time. This technique is called stacking. Gently and smoothly pull the thread through the layers. To end, make a small knot and bury it in the batting.

Machine Quilting

Machine quilting requires an even-feed or walking foot to ensure quilting a straight stitch without distorting the layers, and a darning foot for free-motion or heavily curved stitching.

Use 100% cotton thread or size .004 monofilament thread (clear for light-colored fabrics, smoky for dark fabrics) on the top and cotton in the bobbin. Pre-test stitch length and thread tension using two muslin pieces layered with batting. Adjust as needed.

Choose a quilting strategy. Begin stitching in the middle and work outward, making sure the layers are taut. Roll the edges of the quilt compactly to reveal the area being quilted; reroll as needed. To secure the thread, take 1 or 2 regular-length stitches forward, backward, and continue forward; stitch a few very small stitches and gradually increase to desired length. Trim thread tails.

Stitch "in the ditch" or along the seamline to secure quilt layers while adding subtle texture. Stitch open areas with a design of your choice.

MAKING BINDING STRIPS

Quilt binding can be cut on the bias or straight of grain. Use a continuous strip of bias for a quilt that will be used frequently or has scalloped edges and rounded corners. Refer to "How To Make Continuous Bias" on pages 62 and 63 for making continuous bias binding. For bias or straight-grain double-fold binding, cut 2½"- or 3"-wide strips of fabric and fold in half, wrong sides together.

ATTACHING THE BINDING

Beginning near the middle of any side, align binding and quilt raw edges. Sew to the corner and stop stitching ¼" from the quilt edge; backstitch to secure (an even-feed foot is very helpful). Remove from sewing machine. Fold the binding strip up and back down over itself, aligning raw edges on the second side, and pin in place. Beginning ¼" from the quilt edge (same point where stitching stopped on the first side), sew binding to second side and stop stitching ¼" from next corner edge; backstitch. Remove from sewing machine and continue in the same manner. After sewing all sides, finish using the technique of your choice. Wrap binding around to the back side, using your fingers to manipulate each corner to achieve a miter on both front and back sides. Pin and blindstitch in place.

SIGNING YOUR QUILT

You will want to sign and date your quilt and record other information important to you, such as the quilt's name, your city and state, and the event the quilt commemorates. You may embroider or use permanent ink to record this information on a piece of fabric that you then stitch to the quilt backing, or you may embroider directly on the quilt.

Make Your First Quilt

You can do it! If you can sew a straight line, you can make beautiful quilts, and *McCall's Quilting* will show you how. Whether your style is traditional or modern, colorful or subdued, you'll find projects here too tempting to resist. Go from nervous newbie to confident quilter with this unique 16-pattern collection.

ISBN-13: 978-1-4647-0862-6

51799

△ EAN

9 781464 708626

LEISURE ARTS®
the art of everyday living
www.leisurearts.com

#6036 US $17.99/CAN $21.99

0 28906 06036 2

UPC

MADE IN CHINA

QLT
1007

ULTIMATE STICKER COLLECTION

STAR WARS
THE CLONE WARS

SECRETS OF THE FORCE

MORE THAN **1000** REUSABLE FULL-COLOR **STICKERS**